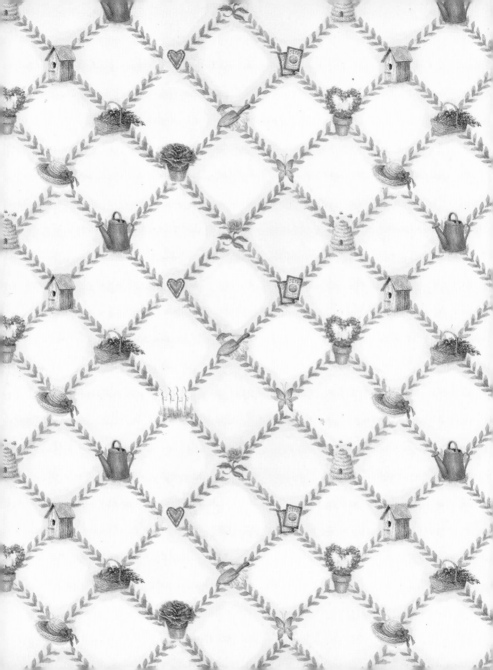

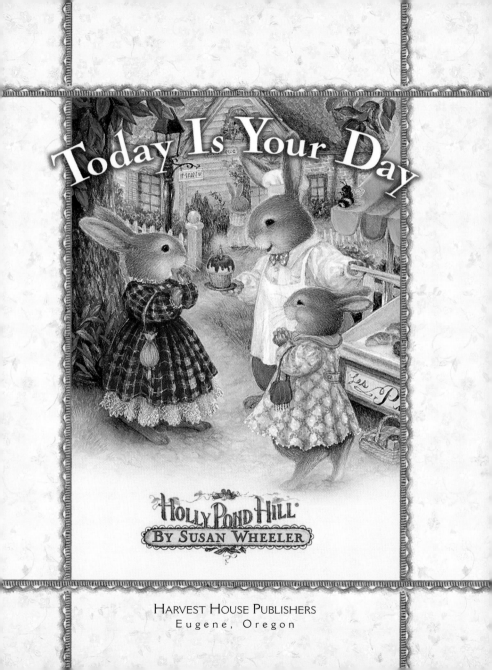

Today Is Your Day

HOLLY POND HILL

BY SUSAN WHEELER

HARVEST HOUSE PUBLISHERS
Eugene, Oregon

Today Is Your Day

Text Copyright © 2001 by Harvest House Publishers
Eugene, Oregon 97402

ISBN 0-7369-0508-1

> InterArt™ Licensing
> P.O. Box 4699
> Bloomington, IN 47402-4699
> 800-457-4045

Design and production by Garborg Design Works, Minneapolis, Minnesota

Harvest House Publishers has made every effort to trace the ownership of all poems and quotes. In the event of a question arising from the use of a poem or quote, we regret any error made and will be pleased to make the necessary correction in future editions of this book.

Printed in Hong Kong

00 01 02 03 04 05 06 07 08 09 / NG / 10 9 8 7 6 5 4 3 2 1

"A little patch I was keeping for my birthday,"

he said; "but after all, what *are* birthdays?

Here today and gone tomorrow..."

A.A. MILNE

*Every gift,
though it be
small, is in
reality great
if given with
affection.*

PINDAR

Love is a gift.
You can't buy
it, you can't
find it, someone
has to give it to
you. Learn to
be receptive of
that gift.
KURT LANGNER

A diplomat is a man who always
remembers a woman's birthday but
never remembers her age.

ROBERT FROST

Celebrate the happiness
that friends are always
giving, make every day
a holiday and celebrate
just living!

AMANDA BRADLEY

Do not regret growing older. *It is a privilege denied to many.*

To keep the heart unwrinkled, to be hopeful, kindly, cheerful, reverent— that is to triumph over old age.

THOMAS B. ALDRICH

ANONYMOUS

Surprise!   H

Remember, the greatest gift is not found in a store
nor under a tree, but in the hearts of true friends.

CINDY LEW

For all the advances in medicine, there is
still no cure for the common birthday.

JOHN HERSCHEL GLENN, JR.

*You can't reach old
age by another
man's road.*

MARK TWAIN

My birthday!—what a different sound
That word had in my youthful ears;
And how each time the day comes round,
Less and less white its mark appears.

THOMAS MOORE

"Mother," said Barnaby,
looking at her steadfastly
as she sat down beside him
after doing so; "is to-day
my birthday?"
"To-day" she answered.
"Don't you recollect it was
but a week or so ago, and
that summer, autumn, and
winter have to pass before it
comes again?"
"I remember that it has
been so till now," said
Barnaby. "But I think to-
day must be my birthday
too, for all that."

CHARLES DICKENS
BARNABY RUDGE

Birthdays
are nature's
way of
telling us
to eat
more cake.

AUTHOR UNKNOWN

You know you are getting old when the candles cost more than the cake.

BOB HOPE

Let nothing disturb thee;

Let nothing dismay thee;

All things pass;

God never changes.

Patience attains

All that it strives for;

He who has God

Finds he lacks nothing.

AUTHOR UNKNOWN

Those who love deeply never grow old.

BENJAMIN FRANKLIN

"How will we give the things?" asked Meg.

"Put them on the table, and bring her in and see her open the bundles. Don't you remember how we used to do on our birthdays?" answered Jo.

"I used to be so frightened when it was my turn to sit in the big chair with the crown on, and see you all come marching round to give the presents, with a kiss. I liked the things and the kisses, but it was dreadful to have you sit looking at me while I opened the bundles," said Beth, who was toasting her face and the bread for tea, at the same time.

LOUISA MAY ALCOTT
LITTLE WOMEN

My dear, I was born to-day—
So all my jolly comrades say:
They bring me music, wreaths, and mirth,
And ask to celebrate my birth.

MATTHEW PRIOR

"This is your birthday. How dare you talk about anything else till you have been wished many happy returns of the day, Tim Linkinwater? God bless you, Tim! God bless you!"

CHARLES DICKENS
Nicholas Nickleby

The twelfth of October was Rose's birthday, but no one seemed to remember that interesting fact, and she felt delicate about mentioning it, so fell asleep the night before wondering if she would have any presents. That question was settled early the next morning, for she was awakened by a soft tap on her face, and opening her eyes she beheld a little black and white figure sitting on her pillow, staring at her with a pair of round eyes very like blueberries, while one downy paw patted her nose to attract her notice. It was Kitty Comet, the prettiest of all the pussies, and Comet evidently had a mission to perform, for a pink bow adorned her neck, and a bit of paper was pinned to it bearing the words,

"For Miss Rose, from Frank."

LOUISA MAY ALCOTT
Eight Cousins

Blowing out candles is good exercise for the lungs.

ANONYMOUS

Some men are born old, and some men never seem so. If we keep well and cheerful, we are always young and at last die in youth even when in years would count as old.

TRYON EDWARDS

LIFE IS WHAT HAPPENS WHEN YOU'RE BUSY EATING BIRTHDAY CAKE.

STEPHEN AXELROD

Do you count your birthdays thankfully?

HORACE

There was a time when a birthday was second only
to Christmas, to our way of thinking. It was as
eagerly anticipated, and the night before was just
as sleepless as Christmas Eve.

R. T. TOWNSEND

27

A Birthday Meditation

Another year is ended,
And still my skies are bright,
For hope and faith are blended,
And all will soon be right.
A song of praise is welling
From out my heart today,
Of the thousand blessings telling
That lie along the way.

MARY INGALLS

A birthday is the
perfect day to let a
special friend know
how much you cherish
her gift of friendsip.

VERONICA CURTIS

29

SURPRISE!

The old believe everything; the
middle-aged suspect everything;
the young know everything.

OSCAR WILDE

The future comes one
day at a time.

AUTHOR UNKNOWN

Most of us can remember a time when a birthday— especially if it was one's own—brightened the world as if a second sun had risen.

ROBERT LUND

A Birthday Wish

Make me content
With fading light;
Give me a glorious sunset
And a peaceful night.

NORMAN B. HALL

33

"I mean, what is an un-birthday present?"
"A present given when it isn't your birthday, of course."
Alice considered a little. "I like birthday presents best,"
she said at last.
"You don't know what you're talking about!"
cried Humpty Dumpty. "How
many days are there in a year?"
"Three hundred and sixty-five," said Alice.
"And how many birthdays have you?"
"One."

LEWIS CARROLL
Alice in Wonderland

*Don't just count your years,
make your years count.*

ERNEST MEYERS

Youth is the gift of nature, but age is a work of art.

GARSON KANIN

Sing a song of birthdays

Full of fun and cheer

And may you keep on having them

For many a happy year.

—ANONYMOUS

This is your birth-day, Tom, and I rejoice
That thus it passes smoothly, quietly:
Many such eves of gently whispering noise
May we together pass, and calmly try
What are this world's true joys,—ere the great Voice
From its fair face shall bid our spirits fly.

JOHN KEATS
WRITTEN TO HIS BROTHER, TOM

A Birthday Walk

A birthday:—and now a day that rose
With much of hope, with meaning rife—
A thoughtful day from dawn to close
The middle day of human life.

JEAN INGLELOW

Wrinkles

should merely

indicate where

smiles have been.

MARK TWAIN

Pa gave Laura a little wooden man he had whittled out of a stick, to be company for her rag doll, Charlotte. Ma gave her five little cakes, one for each year. Mary gave her a new dress for Charlotte. Mary had made the dress herself, when Laura thought she was sewing on her patchwork quilt...

So they went laughing to bed and lay listening to Pa and the fiddle singing. It had been a happy birthday in the little house in the Big Woods.

LAURA INGALLS WILDER

The table is set
The time is near
To celebrate you
And be of good cheer!

GENEVIEVE SMITH

Pleas'd to look forward,
pleas'd to look behind,
And count each birth-day
with a grateful mind.

ALEXANDER POPE

Susan Wh

Believing hear, what

you deserve to hear:

Your birthday as my

own to me is dear...

But yours gives most;

For mine did only lend

Me to the World;

yours gave me a friend.

MARCUS MARTIAL

I think that
I shall never budge
From this cake of frosted fudge;
O, chocolate taste
I love so true,
Nothing else will ever do.

MILTON
HOLLY POND HILL

Real birthdays are not annual affairs.
Real birthdays are the days when
we have a new birth.

RALPH PARLETTE

"Many happy returns of the day,"
said Piglet again.
"Meaning me?"
"Of course, Eeyore."
"My birthday?"
"Yes."
"Me having a real birthday?"
"Yes, Eeyore, and I've brought you a present."
"...Meaning me again?"
"Yes."
"My birthday still?"
"Of course, Eeyore."
"Me going on having a real birthday?"
"Yes, Eeyore, and I brought you a balloon."
"Balloon?" said Eeyore. "You did say balloon?
One of those big coloured things you
blow up? Gaiety, song-and-dance,
here we are and there we are?"

A.A. MILNE
Winnie the Pooh

Though we may prefer to forget
our own birthdays, we like other
people to remember them.

A. G. GARDINER

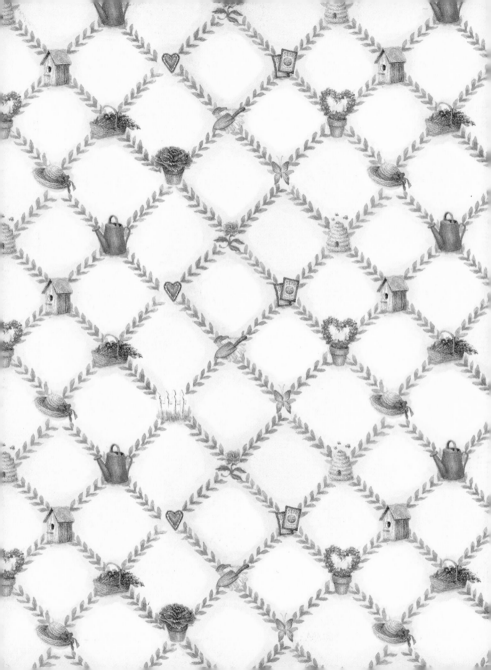